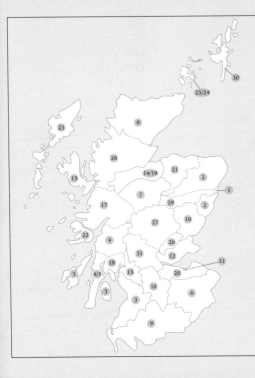

1. Aberd...
2. Aberd...
3. Arran
4. Argyl...
5. Souther...
6. The Borders
7. The Cairngorms
8. Caithness & Sutherland
9. Dumfries and Galloway
10. Dundee & Angus
11. Edinburgh
12. Fife, Kinross & Clackmannan
13. Glasgow
14. Inverness
15. The Isle of Skye
16. Lanarkshire
22. Mull & Iona
23. Orkney
24. Orkney in Wartime
25. The Outer Hebrides
26. The City of Perth
27. Perthshire
28. Ross & Cromarty
29. Royal Deeside
30. Shetland
31. Stirling & The Trossachs

The remaining four books, Caledonia, Distinguished Distilleries, Scotland's Mountains and Scotland's Wildlife feature locations throughout the country so are not included in the above list.

PICTURING SCOTLAND

THE CAIRNGORMS

COLIN NUTT
Author and photographer

NESS PUBLISHING

2 The Cairngorms plateau viewed from the north at Drumchork. The summit of Cairngorm itself is on the left and the Lairig Ghru cuts through the middle of the mountains.

THE CAIRNGORMS

Welcome to the Cairngorms National Park!

Britain's highest and most massive mountain range; its biggest native forests; spectacularly clean rivers and lochs; moorland and farmland and a stronghold for wildlife – this special place offers the warmest of welcomes from the people who live and work here.

The Cairngorms National Park, the largest in Britain, was created in September 2003 and extended in 2010 to a massive 4,528 sq. kilometres. This gave official recognition to the uniqueness of the region: Britain's largest area of arctic mountain landscape, including five peaks over 4000ft/1220m, and one of Europe's biggest nature reserves. It is home to 25% of Britain's endangered birds, animals and plants. The sheer variety of landscape types and usage all add up to great scenic beauty, drama and contrast. Here too are the most extensive patches of remnant Caledonian pinewoods. ('Caledonia', Scotland's Latin-Gaelic name, means 'wooded heights'.)

The unique terrain provides the principal stronghold of several rare birds such as the capercaillie, ptarmigan and Scottish crossbill. The osprey famously re-established itself at Loch Garten in the north of the park and has now spread more widely over Scotland. An abundance of mammals is also present, from the easily observed red deer through the less often seen red squirrel to the elusive pine marten and wild cat. The prospect that any of these *might* be seen adds a frisson of anticipation to an exploration of the Cairngorms' paths and byways. Other furry faces you might encounter belong to otters and badgers; up aloft, that large wingspan could be a buzzard or even a golden eagle.

Pictured from Dornoch beach, Sutherland, about 50 miles to the north, this view shows how the 5
Cairngorms can visually dominate the landscape from even quite distant parts of Scotland.

Within the park are numerous towns and villages such as Aviemore, Ballater, Braemar, Grantown-on-Spey, Kingussie and Newtonmore. These settlements provide further variety and interest to the whole kaleidoscope of images and activity that add up to make the Cairngorms a truly special place. 17,000 people live in the National Park whereas at least 1.4 million people visit the area each year. While this makes tourism the life-blood of the economy, it also represents a major challenge to the ecology of the Cairngorms.

From a distance, the Cairngorms massif is deceptive to the eye. A casual glance may not be held for long by the smoothly rounded uplift of the hills for, disguised by the sheer scale of the range, they appear more hilly than mountainous. And yet the park contains no fewer than 20% of Scottish hills over 3000ft/914m (the Munros). Scotland possesses many mountains that turn the casual glance to a gaze of awe more readily than do these granite mounds at first acquaintance. The Cairngorms make you *work* to discover their dramatic side. For the most part, the drama is hidden from the outside observer. But venture into the glens or climb the mountain paths and see the glacier-work revealed in the scooped corries, the sheer faces of truncated spurs, the near-vertical precipices and fearsome buttresses that line the ice-carved valleys. The greatest of these is the Lairig Ghru, one feature that *is* visible from afar as a V-shaped gash slicing north to south through the heart of the mountains.

This book takes the reader on a circular tour of the region, beginning at Cairngorm Mountain and then proceeding in an anti-clockwise direction. It aims to represent as much in the way of scenery and places of interest as possible so as to convey the immense variety of all there is to be explored. Do enjoy the ride!

The glacial gash of the Lairig Ghru carves its way through the Cairngorms. To its left is Ben Macdui, at 1309m/4295ft the highest point in the Cairngorms and the second-highest mountain in Scotland.

8   A panorama from Creagan Gorm, just north of the main Cairngorms massif. 'Cairngorm' means blue-green hills. The summit of Cairn Gorm itself is on the left, to the right of which is rugged Coire

an t-Sneachda – see following pages. Braeriach (see pages 38-39) is right of centre, above the left-hand **9** end of Loch Morlich (see pages 21-25).

10 A corrie in close-up. This is Coire an t-Sneachda, just west of Cairn Gorm. Corries were the starting-point of the glaciers which gouged the mountain side, leaving precipices like this.

Left: the view from the climb up the corrie wall with the corrie lochan below and Cairn Gorm's **11** summit in the distance. Right: looking upwards reveals the rugged nature of the eroding granite.

12 By contrast, the easy way up (and down!) is by the funicular railway. If you let the train take the strain, you will be able to enjoy the vista from the viewing deck or restaurant at the top.

Busy day on the slopes: the funicular carries its peak volume of passengers on winter days like this **13** when skiers and snowboarders make the most of being able to ride up to 1097m/3600ft.

14 While most skiers stick to the main runs, others like going *off-piste*. Here, an experienced skier sets off into Coire an t-Sneachda, which looks very different from its appearance on p.10.

Some snowboarders also like to brave the uncharted territory of the steep corries.

16 Winter walking in the mountains requires a different level of equipment: these roped-together walkers also use ice axes where necessary and wear hard hats.

A group of climbers can be seen preparing to ascend Fiacaill Buttress. Winter climbing of this nature **17** should only be undertaken by experienced climbers or under the supervision of expert guides.

18 The Cairngorms' plateau is a heavily dissected one, as this scene shows. The three summits are (from nearest) Carn Etchachan, Creagan a Choire Etchachan and Derry Cairngorm.

In different mood and winter mode, a few tiny figures give scale to the scene. In the distance and **19** miles away to the south, Cairn Toul (1291m/4236ft) breaks through the clouds.

20 The view south-east from Cairngorm overlooks Glen Avon, beyond which rises Beinn Mheadhoin (1182m/3878ft), topped with a small tor typical of many Cairngorm summits.

Beautiful Loch Morlich, first seen on p.9, lies in Glen More at the foot of the Cairngorms massif. **21**
Seen on a perfect summer morning it shows off its sandy beach and forest fringes.

22 In stark contrast, here is Loch Morlich on a winter evening. Roughly rectangular, it is a mile or so long and almost a mile across.

Loch Morlich enjoys one of the finest settings of any stretch of water in Scotland, with its backdrop **23** of the north face of the Cairngorm mountains. The moon has the sky all to itself.

24 While this picture takes in a similar stretch of scenery to the previous one, the change of season creates an entirely different impression. In summer, the loch caters for all manner of recreational

activity, including a variety of water sports. A network of surrounding paths allows exploration of
the forest's flora and fauna on foot or by bike.

26 Looking at the mountains from above, classic glacial features such as truncated spurs and hanging valleys are clear to see in this winter aerial view of Loch Avon.

For comparison, here it is from its north-eastern end early on a mid-summer morning, the only time **27** of year when the sun shines right along the loch to the head of the glen.

28 Moving to the head of Loch Avon, Shelter Stone Crag stands tall on the left. At more than 750m above sea level it is one of Scotland's highest lochs, yet at the top of the waterfall on the right

we come to the even higher Loch Etchachan. This view looks north, with the trench of Glen Avon visible in the centre and the summit of Cairn Gorm in the distance. **29**

30 Left: capercaillie. Numbers of this magnificent large grouse are down to around 1,300 birds. Right upper: male ptarmigan in its winter plumage. Right lower: female in summer plumage.

Left: the dotterel is a scarce summer visitor to mountain areas in Scotland, mainly the Cairngorms. **31**
Right: red squirrels remain plentiful for now at least: patience and *quietness* are required to see them!

32 Left: red deer are, if anything, too plentiful, but what a fine sight a stag makes! Right: you can visit the reindeer that have roamed the hills above Glen More since 1952.

The Strathspey Steam Railway has restored Caledonian Railway locomotive No. 828 to working **33** order at its Aviemore works. Here it is, fresh out of the paint shop.

34 Loch an Eilein lies just south of Aviemore, tucked away in Rothiemurchus Forest, a quiet corner of which is seen at dawn on an autumn day.

And on the other side of the loch is the 'Eilein' (island) from which it gets its name. The castle goes back to the 13th century, although what now remains dates to around 1600.

36 From Loch an Eilein one can walk a few miles into the jaws of the Lairig Ghru. The glacier which created it has left some fearsome cliffs such as Lurcher's Crag, seen here.

A little further along the Lairig Ghru, mist and cloud teasingly hides then reveals its secrets. **37**
Across on the far (western) side from where this picture was taken lurk more of the highest peaks . . .

38 . . . such as Braeriach (1296m/4252ft), the northern corries of which have a summer storm brewing above them. Cairngorms' weather is notorious for its habit of changing very suddenly.

At the other end of the year, we see Braeriach sporting its winter coat and looking suitably **39** impressive – if not a little challenging – on a beautifully clear evening as the shadows lengthen.

40 This is in fact a similar view to the one on the previous page, although taken from the north rather than the north-west. It demonstrates very well how the clouds can impart shape-shifting qualities to

the mountains, as it is not easy to reconcile what we see here with the previous image – such is the **41** fascination of mountain watching.

42 From the Black Pinnacle near Braeriach's summit, the Cairngorms show a far more rugged aspect than is apparent from a distance. And now, in contrast to p.19, we see Cairn Toul clearly.

Shifting our gaze to the left (east) of the picture opposite reveals Ben Macdui across the Lairig Ghru. **43**
Visible in both pictures at the end of the ridge is Carn a' Mhaim (1037m/3402ft).

44 Now we turn our attention to the Cairngorms' western ridge, the north end of which is marked by Sgor an Dubh Mor (1111m/3646ft) on the right, with Sgor Gaoith (1118m/3668ft) on the left.

When seen in close-up minus snow, Sgor Gaoith shows it too has its challenging side, in the form of **45** this granite staircase that drops down towards Loch Einich way below.

46 Whichever way you approach, getting to Glen Einich is quite a walk. If climbing via the mountain route from Glen Feshie to Sgor Gaoith, the reward is this dramatic vista down to Loch Einich.

The Cairngorms' west ridge drops down to Glen Feshie on its western side. Here at Feshiebridge, **47** the rapids on the River Feshie are a favourite spot for photographers.

48 It's only a short way from Feshiebridge to Loch Insh, where watersports such as sailing, canoeing, kayaking and windsurfing can all be enjoyed in this superb setting.

For those not looking for such energetic activity, the quieter corners of Loch Insh provide some **49** idyllic spots simply to enjoy the serenity of the surroundings.

50 As the seasons roll round, so inevitably the palette changes and here Loch Insh shows off its autumn colours. Early snow already coats the Cairngorms' western ridge.

The Highland Wildlife Park is situated between Loch Insh and Kingussie. Left: this Amur tiger cub 51 was born at the park. Right: Scottish wild cats also feature among the collection.

52 Continuing south, the planned village of Kingussie was laid out in 1799 at the behest of the Duke of Gordon. The hotel that bears his name stands beyond the Memorial Gardens.

The town's fortunes were boosted by the arrival of the Highland Railway in 1863, the 150th **53** anniversary of which was celebrated in 2013 complete with steam loco and period re-enactments.

54 Returning now to Glen Feshie, in the depths of winter beautiful ice sculptures like this can often be seen in the Feshie and its tributaries. Early in the 19th century Glen Feshie was established

as a destination for deer stalking, causing a detrimental effect on its ecology. From the early 21st C.
an extensive cull has reduced deer numbers in an effort to allow native species to re-grow.

56 This long, wild and glorious glen is not greatly visited, which on the one hand is part of its appeal, but on the other it means that many visitors to the Cairngorms do not see its wonderful landscape.

It more than rewards the walk of approximately four miles each way from the end of the public road
which enables this magical vista to be enjoyed.

58 Ruthven Barracks, just outside Kingussie, is one of four defensible barracks built to police the Highlands after the 1715 Jacobite uprisings. Completed in 1721 on the mound of an earlier castle.

Just south of Kingussie, Newtonmore is home to the Highland Folk Museum which brings to life the **59** domestic and working conditions of earlier Highland peoples. 'Baile Gean' recreates the early 1700s.

60 Among so many aspects of past Highland life recreated at this extensive site, here are, clockwise from top left, Craig Dhu Tweed Shop, Knockbain School, Kirk's Stores and life on the farm.

'Aultlarie' farm steading probably dates from the early 1800s and is interpreted here for the 1930s. **61**
It is the largest *in situ* building on the Museum's site and is often a hive of activity.

62 Continuing southwards, here is a night view of Scotland's second-highest distillery, Dalwhinnie. Founded in 1897 as Strathspey Distillery, its annual capacity is around 2,000,000 litres.

Dalwhinnie is just a few miles from the summit of the Drumochter Pass, overshadowed by several **63** mountains including A'Mharconaich with its long summit ridge, a Munro at 975m/3199ft.

64 The extension of the National Park in 2010 took in northern Perthshire, meaning that the spectacular Falls of Bruar are now within its boundaries. Note the rock arch spanning the water.

The southwards extension of the Park also takes in historic Blair Castle, Headquarters of Europe's last remaining private army, the Atholl Highlanders. **65**

66 To the east, famous Glen Shee is now within the park. In winter the mountains here form another of the skiing areas in the Cairngorms, as can be seen on the mountain top.

Returning to the park's original territories, the lovely Angus Glens are another area of unique **67** character. At the head of Glen Esk is Loch Lee, on this occasion showing its rougher side.

68 Beyond Loch Lee, the many burns that feed it provide delightful cameos like this. This area is quite accessible, requiring a level walk of no more than three miles from the road end.

Traversing the Angus Glens from east to west, next up is 18-mile long Glen Clova. Early snow adds a wintry aspect to this October image. The fertile valley floors are extensively farmed. **69**

70 The road ends at Acharn where the glens divide. The River South Esk heads north into the eastern section of the Cairngorms mountains and paths lead walkers right through to Deeside.

From the same point, Glen Doll takes a more westerly trajectory but also heads into the mountains, **71** which appear impenetrable, but again there are paths to the tops and over to Glen Muick.

72 Glen Prosen lies west of Glen Clova. Although one of the smaller glens it deserves exploration as this panorama illustrates. It is now home to a memorial to Scott of the Antarctic and Dr Edward

Wilson, who stayed at Burnside Lodge in Glen Prosen while planning their ill-fated expedition of 1912. Our journey continues in the outlying flank of the Cairngorms which lies on the horizon.

74 Referred to by some as the White Mounth, this part of the Cairngorms' range is focused on the mountain named Lochnagar, at 1155m/3789ft the highest in this area. Pictured here from Glen Muick.

Loch Muick lies at the head of the glen. The largest loch in the Cairngorms, on a clear day its waters **75** are almost unrealistically blue. Broad Cairn (998m/3274ft) is towards the right.

76 The summit of Lochnagar is the ideal place from which to gain an overview of Royal Deeside, the next stage of our tour. This view looks east towards Braemar.

But first comes the bonny Deeside village of Ballater, still colourful on this October day. Its origins go back to the 13th century, but it was from 1770 that a planned town came into being.

78 Left: Glenmuick Parish Church stands on the village green. Right: The flower beds around the War Memorial front this view which shows Craigendarroch rising to the west of the village.

Ballater grew following the arrival of the railway from Aberdeen in 1866. Although the line was **79** closed in 1966 the Old Royal Station remains active as an information centre and museum.

80 Queen Victoria and Prince Albert built Balmoral Castle from 1853 to 1856. The original building, which they had occupied in the meantime, was then demolished. The castle is open to visitors

from April to July and offers much of interest. The Ballroom houses many items which are normally on display within the castle. The walls are decorated with paintings by Landseer and Carl Haag.

82 Royal Lochnagar Distillery was granted a Royal Warrant of Appointment by Queen Victoria in 1848. It is set in beautiful scenery close to Balmoral Castle. Tours and tastings are available.

Heather is one of the defining plants of the Highlands. This heather garden at Royal Lochnagar **83**
Distillery contains many varieties.

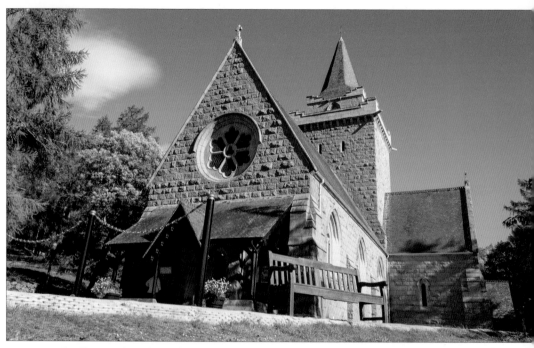

84 West of Ballater is the village of Crathie, whose church (above, opened 1895) has been made famous by royal patronage due to its proximity to Balmoral Castle.

As we continue up Deeside towards Braemar this most appealing up-river view can't fail to catch the **85** eye. The Dee flows for 85 miles from the slopes of Braeriach to Aberdeen.

86 John Erskine, Earl of Mar (1558-1634) started building Braemar Castle in 1628. Although the subject of ongoing restoration it is open to visitors from Easter to autumn.

At 335m/1100ft above sea level, the village of Braemar is the highest and most mountainous parish in the UK. Its location and charm make it a good base from which to explore the area.

88 From the settlement of Inverey west of Braemar, this spectacular winter panorama shows how we have circumnavigated the Cairngorms as now we see Cairn Toul – the peak on the right – from the

south-east, whereas the previous view (p.42) was from the north. The lower summit to the left is the Devil's Point (1004m/3294ft).

90 The annual Braemar Gathering is held on the first Saturday in September and features traditional Highland games such as tossing the caber (left) and parades by marching bands of pipers.

The River Dee meanders through pine forest west of Braemar. On a tranquil evening like this, **91** it's hard to think of anything that better evokes the classic idea of Scottish scenery.

92 A couple of miles further upstream is the Linn ('gorge pool') of Dee. The spectators on the left are looking out for leaping salmon, one of which is seen in the inset picture.

The Dee is joined from the north by Quoich Water, seen here at the Linn of Quoich with the **93** Punchbowl – a curious bowl-shaped depression in the rock – visible to the left of the rapids.

94 From the upper Deeside road near Inverey some impressive mountainscapes can be seen in the distance, especially in winter when the snow makes them look all the more spectacular.

To continue the tour we backtrack down Deeside and head north over the hills to Glen Gairn, **95** seen here looking its summer best with the heather in full bloom.

96 Looking in the opposite direction, in mid-March there is still plenty of snow, although the patchwork patterns in the hillside vegetation that are a distinctive feature of the area are quite clear to see.

Continuing north to Strath Don, Corgarff Castle stands tall in its lonely isolation. Dating back to the 15th century, this fine tower house has an inevitably turbulent history. **97**

98 After several burnings, it was re-fortified after the 1745 rebellion with the addition of the star-shaped outer wall, designed to aid defence by musket.

At the summit of the notorious (in winter) Cockbridge to Tomintoul road is the Cairngorms' third **99** skiing area, Lecht 2090, which in summer is used for Mountain Bike Trails.

100 The attractive village of Tomintoul, planned and built in 1776 around a green square, is the highest village in the Highlands at 356m/1170ft. The elegant statue is set above the drinking fountain.

Journeying onwards around the north-eastern edge of the Cairngorms on the A939 presents this **101** view of Strathavon (the head of which we first saw on p.27) near the settlement of Fodderletter.

102 The A939 delivers us to the elegant town of Grantown-on-Spey, laid out in 1766 at the direction of Sir James Grant. Close by the town's stylish architecture is this lovely park.

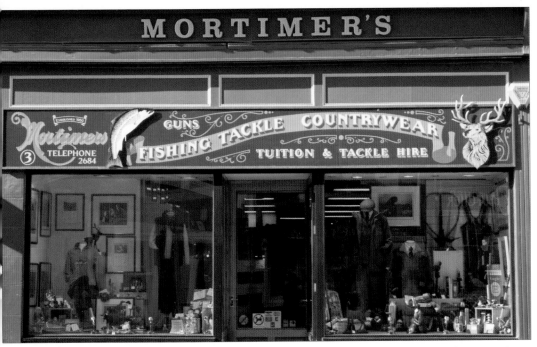

A delightfully traditional shop front in Grantown reflects the many outdoor pursuits to be enjoyed **103**
in the vicinity. Grantown's Museum is also well worth a visit.

104 Looking every bit the Arctic-alpine wilderness that it is, the Cairngorms' mountain landscape at sunset on a winter's day is both beautiful and forbidding. The top station of the funicular catches

the dying light and gives a sense of scale to the panorama. The central mountain area is classified as a rare habitat within the UK, with flora and fauna adapted to its extreme climate.

106 Taken from Broomhill about half way between Grantown and Aviemore, this view across Strathspey gives a good idea of the mixture of landscape types within the park.

At Carrbridge the River Dulnain (a tributary of the Spey) flows under the remains of the old **107** packhorse bridge built in 1717. Heavy rain has raised the water level dramatically.

108 The osprey became extinct in Scotland in 1899 but re-established itself here at Loch Garten in 1959. Today an RSPB observation centre enables visitors to watch them.

The Strathspey Railway runs steam and other heritage trains between Aviemore and Broomhill. **109**
On the way the trains stop here at Boat of Garten.

110 With our circular tour almost complete, we pause for a look at little-known Loch Pityoulish on the minor road from Coylumbridge to Nethy Bridge. The ever-present mountains loom beyond.

With the sun about to say goodnight to the distant summit of Cairn Gorm, it's time, briefly, **111** for some extraordinary clouds to take centre stage. These clouds are made by the mountains.

Published 2014 by Ness Publishing, 47 Academy Street, Elgin, Moray, IV30 1LR. Reprinted 2017
Phone 01343 549663 www.nesspublishing.co.uk
(First edition published 2008 under the title *The Cairngorms: a pictorial souvenir*)

All photographs © Colin and Eithne Nutt except pp.7 & 26 © Scotavia Images; pp.30 (left and right upper) & 108 (inset)
© Mark Hicken; pp.4, 31 (right) & 32 (left) © Charlie Phillips; p.32 (right) © Cairngorm Reindeer Herd;
p.51 (both) © Alex Riddell; p.60 (lower right) © Highland Folk Museum; pp.80 & 81 © Balmoral Estates

Text © Colin Nutt
ISBN 978-1-906549-36-7

Front cover: Corrie an t-Sneachda and Cairn Lochan in winter; p.1: Cairngorms National Park boundary sign; p.4: pine
martens once again inhabit the Cairngorms; this page: ducks on Loch Morlich; back cover: Royal Bridge, Ballater

For a list of websites and phone numbers please turn over > > > >

Websites and phone numbers (where available) of featured places in alphabetical order:

Angus Glens: www.angusglens.co.uk
Aviemore: www.visitaviemore.co.uk
Ballater: www.visitballater.com
Balmoral Castle: www.balmoralcastle.com (T) 01339 742534
Blair Castle: www.blair-castle.co.uk (T) 01796 481207
Braemar Castle: www.braemarcastle.co.uk (T) 01339 741219
Braemar Gathering: www.braemargathering.org (T) 01339 755377
Braemar: www.visitcairngorms.com/braemar
CairnGorm Mountain (funicular railway): www.cairngormmountain.com (T) 01479 861261
Cairngorm Reindeer Centre: www.cairngormreindeer.co.uk (T) 01479 861228
Cairngorms National Park Authority: www.cairngorms.co.uk (T) 01479 873535
Carrbridge: www.carrbridge.com
Corgarff Castle: www.historic-scotland.gov.uk (T) 01975 651460
Crathie Church: www.royal-deeside.org.uk (T) 01339 755467
Dalwhinnie Distillery: www.discovering-distilleries.com 01540 672219
Glenmore Forest Park: www.forestry.gov.uk (T) 01479 861220
Glenshee Ski Centre: www.ski-glenshee.co.uk (T) 01339 741320
Grantown-on-Spey: www.grantownonline.co.uk
Highland Folk Museum: www.highlandfolk.com (T) 01540 673551
Highland Wildlife Park: www.kincraig.com (T) 01540 651270
Kingussie: www.kingussie.co.uk
Lecht 2090: www.lecht.co.uk (T) 01975 651440
Loch Garten Osprey Centre: www.rspb.org.uk (T) 01479 831476
Loch Insh Water Sports: www.lochinsh.com (T) 01540 651272
Old Royal Station: www.royal-deeside.org.uk (T) 01339 755467